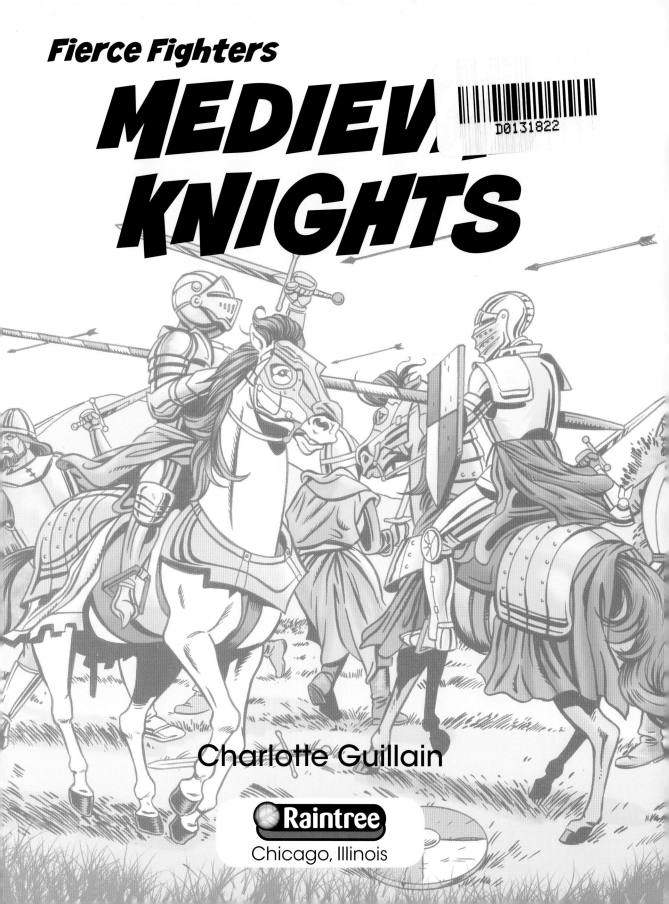

Fierce Fighters
MEDIEVAL KNIGHTS

Charlotte Guillain

Raintree
Chicago, Illinois

www.heinemannraintree.com
Visit our website to find out
more information about
Heinemann-Raintree books.

To order:

☎ Phone 888-454-2279

🖥 Visit www.heinemannraintree.com
to browse our catalog and order online.

Edited by Rebecca Rissman, Nancy Dickmann,
and Catherine Veitch
Designed by Joanna Hinton-Malivoire
Original illustrations © Capstone Global Library 2010
Original illustrations by Miracle Studios
Picture research by Tracy Cummins
Production by Victoria Fitzgerald
Originated by Capstone Global Library
Printed and bound in China by Leo Paper Products Ltd

14 13 12 11 10
10 9 8 7 6 5 4 3 2 1

**Library of Congress Cataloging-in-
Publication Data**
Guillain, Charlotte.
  Medieval knights / Charlotte Guillain.
    p. cm. -- (Fierce fighters)
  Includes bibliographical references and index.
  ISBN 978-1-4109-3763-6 (hc) -- ISBN 978-1-4109-
3771-1 (pbk.) 1. Knights and knighthood--Juvenile
literature. 2. Civilization, Medieval--Juvenile literature. I.
Title.
  CR4513.G85 2010
  940.1--dc22
                        2009030853

Acknowledgments
We would like to thank the following for permission to
reproduce photographs: Age Fotostock p. **16** (© Thomas
Frey), Alamy p. **27** (© United Archives GmbH), Corbis
pp. **13** (© P Deliss/Godong), **14** (© Bettmann), **19**
(© Blue Lantern Studio); Getty Images pp. **7** (Johannes
Simon), **11** (Edmund Blair Leighton), **17** (Dorling
Kindersley), **22** (Italian School); Heinmann Raintree
pp. **28 top** (Karon Dubke), **28 bottom** (Karon Dubke),
29 top (Karon Dubke), **29 bottom** (Karon Dubke);
Shutterstock p. **26** (© William Attard McCarthy); The
Art Archive pp. **18** (Bibliothèque de l'Arsenal Paris /
Kharbine-Tapabor / Coll. Jean Vigne), **21** (Musée Condé
Chantilly / Gianni Dagli Orti), **24** (Musée Thomas
Dobrée Nantes / Gianni Dagli Orti), **25** (Centre Jeanne
d'Arc Orléans / Gianni Dagli Orti); The Bridgeman Art
Library pp. **9** (Private Collection / © Look and Learn);
The Bridgeman Art Library International p. **15** (© Wallace
Collection, London, UK).

Front cover photograph of knights charging reproduced
with permission of Miracle Studios.

Some words are shown in bold, **like this**. You can find
out what they mean by looking in the glossary.

Contents

Knight Fight

Place: France
Date: 1400s

England is at war with France. English soldiers shoot arrows at the French to start a new battle. Then **warriors** on horseback **gallop** onto the battlefield. Their swords and **armor** clash as the fight begins.

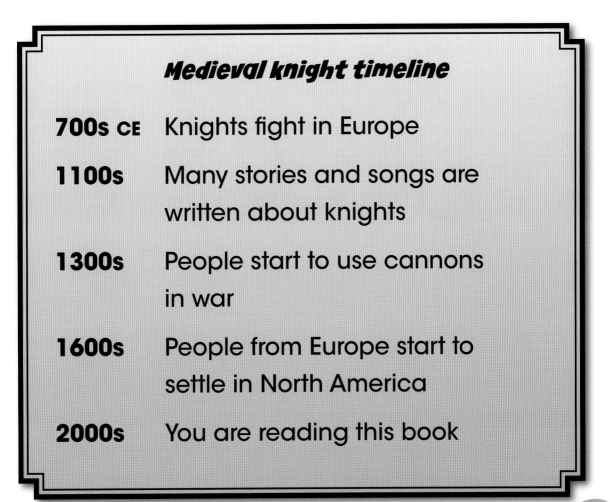

Medieval knight timeline

700s CE	Knights fight in Europe
1100s	Many stories and songs are written about knights
1300s	People start to use cannons in war
1600s	People from Europe start to settle in North America
2000s	You are reading this book

Who Were Medieval Knights?

Medieval knights lived in parts of Europe hundreds of years ago. They wore heavy **armor**, carried swords, and rode horses into battle. There were many wars at that time. Knights fought for their king or another ruler.

Medieval Europe

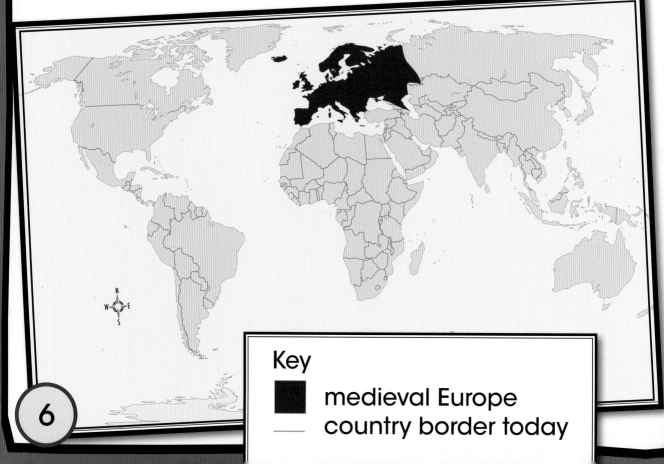

Key

■ medieval Europe

___ country border today

DID YOU KNOW?

Fighting on piggyback was good training for fighting on horseback.

Becoming a Knight

Many boys became knights because their fathers were knights. They started working as a **page** for a knight when they were about seven years old.

DID YOU KNOW?
A page did jobs for the knight and learned to fight.

When a page was 14 years old, he could become a **squire**. A squire looked after the knight's horses and cleaned his weapons and **armor**. He helped his master before a battle and watched him fight.

DID YOU KNOW?

If a knight's armor or weapons broke, the squire had to run out into the battle with new ones.

This squire is being
made a knight.

A Knight's Weapons

Knights fought on horseback with a long **lance**. A lance is a long wooden pole with a strong metal point. In battle a knight used a lance to knock other knights off horses.

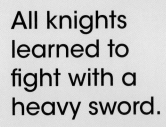

All knights learned to fight with a heavy sword.

Knights also used small **daggers** and axes to hurt their enemies in battle. The **mace** was a wooden stick with metal spikes at the top. A knight used a mace to smash open an enemy's armor.

warhammer

mace

DID YOU KNOW?

Knights also used big hammers called **warhammers** to knock out their enemies.

A knight had to buy his own suit of **armor**. It was made of metal and could weigh as much as a six-year-old child! Some armor was made of small metal rings in chains. Other armor was made of strong steel plates.

DID YOU KNOW?
A knight's horse also wore some armor.

17

Practice Fighting

Knights practiced fighting when they were not at war. They fought one another and fought in **tournaments**. **Jousting** was when two knights rode their horses toward each other. They tried to knock each other off their horses with **lances**.

DID YOU KNOW?

Sometimes knights were killed or badly hurt when they jousted.

Knights also fought in pretend battles at **tournaments**. Many people came to watch these fights. It was just a game, but the knights could be very rough. Sometimes knights died.

DID YOU KNOW?

Some pretend battles were called mêlées (say *mel-ay*). Sometimes people came to watch the fighting.

War Horses

A knight could not go to war without his horse. A good war horse cost a lot of money. They had to be fit and strong to carry a knight in heavy **armor**.

DID YOU KNOW?
Some knights trained their horses to kick out at their enemies.

Medieval Women

Medieval women could not become knights. Most women had to look after the home and their children. A rich woman could ask a knight to wear her scarf at a **tournament**.

DID YOU KNOW?

Joan of Arc was a teenage girl who led the French army into battle. Her enemies took her prisoner and burned her to death.

The End of Medieval Knights

Knights were the fiercest fighters in Europe for hundreds of years. Then life changed and wars became different. People stopped fighting in **armor** with swords and started using **cannons**.

cannon

These days we only see knights in films and stories.

Knight Activity

Make a medieval knight's shield

You will need:
- large piece of thick cardboard
- scissors
- pencil
- paints
- glue

1. Draw a shield shape on the cardboard and cut it out.

2. Paint the front of the shield. Look at the shields in the pictures in this book to get some ideas.

3. Attach a strip of cardboard to the back so you can hold your shield.

You are ready to go into battle!

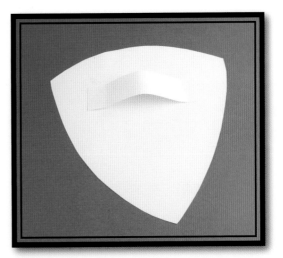

Glossary

armor metal clothing knights wore to protect them in battle

cannon big gun that fired a metal ball called a cannonball

dagger small sword

gallop fastest way for a horse to run

joust contest between two knights on horseback

lance pole used by a knight to knock other knights off their horses

mace club that sometimes had spikes on it

medieval a time in history, from the 400s to the 1400s

page young boy who served a knight

squire teenage boy who was training to be a knight

tournament contest for knights

warhammer large hammer with long handle used as a weapon

warrior fighter

Find Out More

Books

Martin, Michael. *Knights*. Mankato, Minn.: Capstone Edge Books, 2007.

Nobleman, Marc Tyler. *Knight*. Chicago: Heinemann-Raintree, 2008.

Websites

library.thinkquest.org/10949/fief/medknight.html
Learn about becoming a knight, armor, and tournaments.

Places to visit

The Metropolitan Museum of Art
www.metmuseum.org/explore/knights/title.html

Visit the Arms and Armor galleries at the museum to find out see the armor knights wore and learn more about it.

Find out

Where did a boy go to train as a page?

Index